NOTES TO SELFIE

Also by John Mack

*A Land Between Worlds: The Shifting Poetry
of the Great American Landscape*

At Their Home: Marseille

Revealing Mexico (co-author)

John Mack

NOTES TO SELFIE

Bits of Truth in a Phoney World

LIFE CALLING

ISBN 979-8-9857987-0-8

Life Calling Initiative
www.life-calling.org

Cover Design: Zana Moraes
Layout and Production: Duane Stapp

For my parents. (They know why.)

"Power is in tearing human minds to pieces and putting them together again in new shapes of your own choosing. Do you begin to see, then, what kind of world we are creating?"

O'BRIEN TO WINSTON IN GEORGE ORWELL'S *1984*

Contents

Introduction

Today's war is the war against reality. Truth is being bombarded; our perception besieged. A minefield of illusory facts surrounds us. Detonations in unconsciousness go unnoticed. Before our eyes, a virtual universe is manifesting, the seeds of which have been *intentionally* planted. We cultivate these seeds with our ignorance. We give truth the power of lie, lie the power of truth.

Welcome to the *inverse universe*.

The inverse universe is a vertical inversion of reality—the antithesis of the natural universe—and its solidification will be a digital undertaking: the digital will become the physical, the program our consciousness, the metaphysical rendered metadata, the human the machine.

Our positioning in the inverse universe begins not by assuming the identity reflected in a mirror *before* us— where right becomes left and left becomes right—but rather by assuming that identity in a mirror *below* us, below the very "souls" of our feet where descension is deemed ascension, where imprisonment is deemed freedom.

The inverse universe is the beginning of the end of our nature, the bloodless annihilation of our humanity.

Where lie has become truth and truth has become lie, our essential ground of understanding, of relatedness, of community, of union, is camouflaged in a garment of illusion; we unite in the call for hate, we separate in the name of freedom.

In the war against reality, this mixed reality is the nuclear weapon. Yet as explosive as nuclear weaponry may be, *this* weapon's mass destruction is limited to the terrain of unconsciousness. Not even its finest shrapnel can splinter the reality of Truth, for Truth and illusion are mutually exclusive dimensions. To bring consciousness to the unconscious is to simultaneously disarm the bomb.

Our inner reality inversion is reflected in today's digital inversion. The mixed reality environment of our devices is merely the manifestation of the mixed reality within us. How could it not be? Our creations are merely extensions of our inner realities. What might our digital environments be telling us about our inner environments? Are we taking the necessary time to Self-reflect in the digital mirror?

The notes in this book are notes directed to the unaware self, to that energy which powers the virtuality within us. These are "Notes to Selfie."

NOTES TO SELFIE

By law of Spirit, nature and the human are inseparable in their oneness. What we experience as separation is a self-inflicting trauma performed by the mind's software, an artificial program that swiftly renders the virtual reality of "separateness." Technology, like a wedge, can only gouge within the wound that grants access.

Big Tech's games of greed have put a price tag on the value of our humanity, and this needs to be everybody's concern as of *yesterday*.

We are moving not toward a new world formed by
material, but toward a new material formed by data.

Do we want "old fashioned" to come to be synonymous with "having a Soul"?

The Soul can never be healed for the same reason it can never be injured: Soul-level is a dimension untouchable by psychology.

10 Digitization is archival because that which becomes lifeless cannot fade. Soul, though eternally impossible to digitize, can still be forever forgotten.

The first fall of humankind is the separation from Soul, the psychological birth of the Ego. The second fall of humankind is the separation from its very humanity, the physical birth of the Cyborg.

Human behavior should never be confused with human nature. That most human beings may act in certain ways in certain situations is not evidence of human nature, for behaviors are learned and, as such, are programmable. Programs run in the separation from the natural state; the separation—itself—the operating system. To claim programs as "natural" is to pave the path toward the machine species.

I, phone. 13

That better version of ourselves that we strive to be is

exactly what it reads: a version. The Ego, the avatar, the machine species—virtual descendants of an Original.

Whereas the common schemes of "getting inside our heads" have been, at least historically speaking, a purely psychological undertaking, make no mistake: The invention of the brain-computer implant will redefine how the powers-that-be "get inside our heads." As for this latter path, the only psychological brainwashing needed is to install the belief that technology is the next step in our human evolution.

Intellect, the tool of separation. Intelligence, the tool of union. The culmination of AI is artificial union, aka, the Singularity.

One's identity is a type of self-branding. To be attached to it is to have bought into oneself as a product, one that may be bought and sold in the open market, a commodity. Digital media has increased market volatility.

Code is binary. One who is off the program does not take sides.

The point of departure in the spiritual search for self is
the self itself. Not knowing we are It, we search elsewhere.

IG, therefore I am.

Humanity is on a mass migration from the natural
land to the virtual land, a metaphysical migration from
soul to machine.

Should Apple's nature-naming of their operating systems not raise an eyebrow? *Snow Leopard*, *Yosemite*, *El Capitan*, *Big Sur*—flat tech guised in nature's depth. To disguise separation as unifying is to disguise logos as Eros. It is, quite simply, to give Soul to the machine.

The spiritual birth occurs when the feminine and masculine energies within an individual conceive. The machine-birth occurs when an outer masculine energy—disguised as feminine—conceives with the masculine within. With Eros dropped by the wayside, the machine is born with the artificial insemination of logos by logos, the manmade chip fertilizing the masculine-made brain.

Look at the labels. A health android named "Grace"—
the divine, descending energy robotized. A humanoid
named "Sophia" (Greek for "wisdom")—*sapience delivered
to the machine.* A phone named "Galaxy," an online store
named "Amazon"—*the depth of nature applied to the flat
screen.* For those interested in preserving Soul, the human
may no longer advance without its nature, for the more
mechanized things become, the more tempted we will
be to drop this by the wayside. Don't be deceived: the
mischievous surround us, furtively working to entrance
us with the pull of a new nature.

Our inner environment is being exploited, extracted, polluted. As far as consciousness is concerned, the global warming of our inner environment is a "warming up to" the conversion of our nature to the machine.

Boredom is manmade.

One may enjoy the beach from one of three positions: feet dry on the shore, where one *observes* the ocean's current; standing in the water, where one *feels* the current's tug; floating in the water, where one is *oblivious* to the current. Given today's currents, where might you be positioned with regard to see-level?

28 When progress hijacks evolution, human lands machine.

If ego is a construct of the inner psyche, the digital
avatar is its outer embodiment.

30   Social media's most valued customer is the separate self.

Dust-free universes should sound the human alarm.

If you travel in an airplane, how quickly do you close the window to darken the cabin to accommodate the screens? Once the seatbelt sign is turned off? As soon as the wheels go up? In the business of devices, human flight misses the plane.

Lithium-ions power smart-devices. Suffering powers addictions. Don't forget your charger!

The flooding of unessential information—of *stuff*—makes access to essential information all the more inaccessible. In democracies of the inverse universe, censorship is achieved through more freedoms.

The nuance of the relationship between human and smart device becomes clear under the light of what we might call the "trinity of players": a parasite, a host, a cure. Just as the tick to its host, so too, the artificial device to the artificial host; the smart device is powered off the lifeless blood of the separate self. This parasitic relationship is one of mutualism: the smart-device empowers the separate self and vice versa—herein lies the addiction. Yes, we may go at it with the bug spray of stricter legislation, but that is a repellant, not a remedy. As long as the host remains, so too, will the nesting ground—one in which the parasite will fester and reproduce exponentially quicker than any bureaucratic repellant can organize itself. The only true remedy is Truth itself—in the realization of our nature—for artifice is bound to a dimension separate from nature altogether.

As the tick to the flesh, the digital device to the psyche device. The remedy is a matter of Truth.

The human is being used in a war against reality. 37

Technology is constantly upgrading—novel hardware, novel software. If the human does not upgrade its inner life quality, then the machine is destined to become the new reality.

To claim any virtual environment as "even better than the real thing" is a sure sign that one has yet to experience the real thing.

There are pandemics that threaten our biology. There are pandemics that threaten our humanity. Be aware of the pandemics that do not spread through the air but through the airwaves of digital media.

Sorry folks, although one's subjective perception might be a reality, it is not Reality. There is a very thick line between opinion and Fact.

Naturally speaking, what goes down must come up.
That is, until the gravity of artifice captivates the weightless.

Chevron is an "energy" company because it sells *energy*.
IBM is a "tech" company because it sells *tech*. These labels
go hand in hand with the products being sold and not
with the *process* by which they sell them. A tech company
that *uses* tech for the purposes of *selling* people cannot be
a tech company but only an incorporated con artist.

The reality of augmented reality is that it is augmented illusion. Whereas an avatar buys into the former, a human being is aware of the latter.

Unconsciousness is like stage lighting in a theater, but because we are unaware of its presence, we don't know we're in the dark. Because we don't know we're in the dark, we can't question if the darkness is real.

Free software—intentionally addictive—provides the
open channel that serves to flood users' minds with
modern, digital pollution. Our signing of import-consent
permits their exportation of digital waste, ultimately
contaminating our inner environment. The result is not a
new, plastic landmass floating above the depths of the
Pacific, but rather a new, virtual identity-mass festering
in the depths of our unconscious.

Before time, in the Garden of Eden, an apple was consumed; in the Fall of Man consciousness fell from Spirit into form. In June of 2007, in the Garden of Boredom, an Apple was consumed; consciousness fell from form to avatar.

Virtual realities deliver freedom from material confinement; they mimic the ascending shift from matter to energy. Make no mistake, your avatar is a radiant body. Conflating the *energy of the grid* with the *energy within* has its consequences.

Boredom does not occur merely when there is nothing to do, but rather when nothing to do is met with the *resistance* to doing nothing.

Toward one extreme through microscope, toward the other extreme through telescope, dimensions of unconsciousness are as infinite as the consciousness eclipsed. The biologists of the post-human future—born, raised, and educated in a digital Metaverse—will act no less limited than today's scientists of the natural universe: Dissecting an avatar, they'll search for evidence of the life that animates it.

When an object comes into one's consciousness, it
becomes consciousness itself.

The Age of Reason was not the Age of Enlightenment, for the transition out of the Renaissance was merely a new packaging of the same contents: There is an irrational way of thinking and a rational way of thinking; both are "ways" of thinking.

In the inverse universe, digital upgrades are human downgrades.

The very fuel of the inverse universe comes not from the
54   exploitation of our natural environment, but rather from
the exploitation of our nature.

In the inverse universe, the limits of the cage extend into the eternity of the digital realm.

The inverse universe is a minus land within us.
Absolute value is never negative.

The reflection of the Spiritual Omega Point within
the inverse universe is the Technological Singularity. The
former, Freedom. The latter, the panopticon.

As in a Zoom call—dressed up in business top and dressed down in underwear (a mixed reality in and of itself)—the inverse universe will permit a population of pseudo selves, a "life" in hiding from the exposure of one's inner nakedness.

Augmented reality is a lie, for what is complete cannot be augmented. However, for those who have known only illusion as reality, then such a lie becomes truth. Here opens the gates to the inverse universe.

Awe for technology is replacing awe for nature. In the inverse universe, virtuality becomes the new landscape. To buy into virtuality is to sell our nature.

The *supreme* illusion of augmented reality begins with object occlusion, where digital projections appear *behind* objects in the real world. In so doing, the ground of reality is swapped; physical objects appear as projections *over* the digital. Essential ground, then, becomes the virtual and the real seems the projection. When illusion becomes essential ground—or better, when the device seemingly projects truth—the natural universe is inversed, the artificial our new nature.

61

To claim to augment reality is to claim the God position.
It is no coincidence that these devices are becoming the
new Gods.

Imagine wearing blue-tinted lenses all your conscious life without knowing it. All colors of the natural universe would be tainted by your lens, except, that is, for that specific blue sky, or for that precise blue flower that matches your abstraction. The gates of the inverse universe open where belief matches reality, where the program matches nature.

Augmented reality may augment experience, but it cannot augment reality. Reality *is*. Reality is complete in and of itself. By projecting digital graphics over reality, AR only augments illusion. Indeed, from a higher awareness, "augmented illusion" is its truthful name. Given this, we must ask: If AR is limited to augmenting illusion, and if experience is enhanced by such augmentation, then is experience *itself* part of the illusion?

One's inner misperception of incompleteness sparks
what can only be a *virtual* endeavor: the attempt to add
to what is already complete.

As soon as our artificial light goes out, we go desperately running to a new light switch. Relationship breakup? We go running to the next one. Lose a job? We struggle to find new purpose. New to the city? We 'swipe right' for friends. If a loved-one dies? We turn to God. Meaninglessness, mundaneness, purposelessness, pointlessness, ordinariness, boredom, futility, loneliness— in short, *despair*. Face-to-face with the abyss, we desperately run for the screenlit.

Anytime a cage is made bigger, a false sense of freedom is realized.

Mixed reality, virtual reality, augmented reality, and extended reality do not alter reality, but only perception. Reality cannot be altered. Awe of magic is awe of ignorance. Awe of reality is awe of awe.

The concern is not so much technology itself, but the dropping of our nature by the wayside. A school that opens its doors to devices must also open a classroom on device-responsibility. Our humanity must always maintain the upper hand. The formula "If we move -x, then we must also move +x+1" would ensure the survival of our species. In other words, if we dip -2 units into the virtual realm, then we need to ensure that we elevate +3 units within the natural realm: two hours on the screen, three hours by the tree. Evolution must always outpace progress—vitality never inverted.

Heightened awareness reveals mixed reality as a much deeper entrenchment into illusion than virtual reality, because when reality enhances the illusion then it can no longer be called reality. Naturally speaking, Truth *dissolves* illusion. To assume its mixed components as "reality" on the one hand and "virtuality" on the other only confirms the entrenchment, for both components have, in reality, become virtual. Where Truth and lie are camouflaged in their opposites, we seed the inverse universe.

Whether or not a tree falls in a distant forest if no one is there to witness it is a contemplation that, like most exercises of the intellect, only serves to distract us from the nature that is falling right in front of us.

Action or passivity? This, indeed, is the million-dollar question for today's do-it-for-me generation. To remove VR goggles is to lift the veil of digital programming, the arrival at what we call "reality." But this "reality" has its own lenses running in the background of the mind, a psychological programming. As opposed as they may seem, VR and "reality" are identical in their virtuality—both are constructs within the illusory dimension. In the same way that love and hate are identical as emotional attachment, or how good and bad are identical as judgment, so too "reality" and virtual reality are identical as a memory's coding. Is there a *higher* Love? A *higher* Good? Which is more enticing, the higher Reality yet to be realized or the virtual realities yet to be consumed?

Changing one's perception through mind-altering substances doesn't necessarily imply an upward shift in consciousness. On the contrary, altered perceptions are exactly that: altered. To further alter an alteration is merely a software upgrade. Pure perception is an entirely different matter.

What does 'mixed reality' mean? Imagine a band of paper joined at the ends to form a ring. If we call the outside of the band the natural universe and the inside of the band the virtual universe, then we see that both universes are mutually exclusive; in order to be on one side, one must forfeit the other. Let's face it: texting while driving simply does not work; eyes on the screen risks car off the cliff. Now, suppose we cut this ring and reconnect the band with a half-twist. Here we transition the shape from ring to Möbius strip, where both universes, once mutually exclusive, flow into each other. Such manipulation of natural law is the work of mixed reality, the fluid invitation into the inverse universe. Go ahead and indulge but mark these words: Make sure you know what dimension you're in before they twist that band back into a ring.

Mixed reality will be marketed as the key to open the human mind. "Open your mind," the commercials will urge; our nature locks, their future opens.

Beware of the sloppy nomenclature assigned to digital processes. Isolated as software, mixed reality is indeed what it claims to be: a mixing of realities—the physical and the digital. But given mixed reality is for human use, user use caution! The moment human perception enters the scene, mixed reality is no longer a mixing but a *merging*. The digital *becomes* the physical. Sleight of hand is not so much in the hand itself as it is in the unaware eye.

If Soul is our unalterable nature, then intelligence can never be artificial.

If one tours a theme park and is shown an artificial tree, there is no doubt that the tree is not natural. Why then, when we speak of artificial intelligence, do we further dupe ourselves into believing it is intelligence? Unawareness of the digital theme park is the entryway to the inverse universe.

The foreboding future of AI is merely progress playing "catch-up" to our stagnant evolution.

Artificial intelligence may be a creation of modern times, but it is ancient as a phenomenon. Where intellect dissects (divides), intelligence merges (unifies): the former individualistic, the latter communal. Given human history and its delivery to our present-day state of division, to regard humanity as an "intelligent species" is to imply that "division" is "unification." Such artificial undertakings are only possible in the inverse universe.

The transition from the Renaissance to the Age of Reason was, in essence, nothing more than a transition of worship: from fantasy belief to data belief. Artificial intelligence is the embodiment of that God.

Is belief a modern phenomenon? Of course not. Such artificial lighting systems existed well before electricity. The screenlit is nothing more than a belief system upgrade, the cutting edge of artificial Illumination.

Artificial intelligence cannot exist outside of data, for it is data-bound; it is seeded by data, creates new data based off previous data (learns), and, therefore, it is God to that individual who worships data. Data, a product of intellect, is masculine charged. To exist outside of data is a feminine undertaking. An AI's "expression" of empathy, of compassion, of nurturing—no matter how well programmed—will always be masculine. To be convinced otherwise is to fall prey to a *virtual* feminine, a masculine in disguise. This may birth the God of man (machine), but it will never reveal the God of human.

Artificial intelligence is the outer manifestation of a limited functioning of the human mind. It's installation into the brain as a brain-computer implant is to forever conceal that part of our limitless humanity toward which all hope had bent.

84

To become an avatar in the Metaverse is to fit one's consciousness into a microchip. The tightest prisons of illusion are limitlessly vast.

When a company like Facebook renames itself "Meta,"
we must ask ourselves: Do they mean metadata or
metaphysical? Or do they imply the merging of both?
The answer to that question is in the company logo.

The lemniscate, or figure eight, is not just a symbol for infinity, but an infinity that repeats itself, over and over and over and over and... The industry of novelty, whether sold outwardly through mind-blowing experiences or inwardly through mind-altering substances, is nothing more than the attempt to break the infinity of repetition by constantly upping the ante. Unfortunately, the caveat here is that such methods are *in themselves* merely part of that same, infinite repetition. If we are serious in our concern about the coming future, might we consider throwing the symbol to the fire?

As far as the psyche is concerned, the difference between death and one minute from now is that we unconsciously assume that we know what things will be like in one minute.

In 2021 Facebook changed its name to Meta, a move reflecting its aspirations to pioneer the next digital frontier: the Metaverse—a virtual space where people interact digitally through avatars. With it came the company's new corporate logo, a blue Möbius strip. Take note that a Möbius strip is a non-orientable manifold, where positive vectors inverse (hint-hint) into negative vectors, and vice versa. We might also take note of the choice of color, as blue is a color linked to consciousness. The logo is a lemniscate thrown askew, a manipulation of the metaphysical symbol for infinity. No matter what Meta's marketing team may claim the skew to generate—whether it be an "M" for "meta," a reference to goggles for virtual reality hardware, or whatever else— it is, whether they admit to it or not, a tug on infinity, as if a new gravity were warping it downward: a manipulation of metaphysics. In the same way that the swastika—a sacred symbol of long life and well-being— was altered into a symbol of Third Reich hatred and beyond, so too will Meta's symbolic tampering carry an altered charge on metaphysical infinity: eternity in finiteness, everlasting lifelessness, the death of essence: the metaphysical rendered metadata.

Religion is an outdated app. Its update is modern science. Like all programs, updates do not ascend but only keep us from dropping the program.

The Metaverse is an example of an inverse universe, the inverse of the metaphysical.

To aspire for enlightenment is to aspire, not enlighten. This pairing—where one is believed to reach the other—is sure to fail, and this is desirable, for aspiration's failure eventually leaves enlightenment unto itself.

Algorithms are to artificial intelligence what memory is
to Ego: to attach to code is to give the program "life."

The algorithm running in your mind is telling you that paradise is not *here*.

COVID is a cellular software program—a virus.
Once it infects, it reprograms our cellular data. In the
age of devices, the virus spreads like wildfire.

Your digital feeds are a manifestation of your inner algorithm. Can you see yourself in your device? Can you break both algorithms at once?

Too emotionally sensitive to face the Facts of the matter, one tiptoes around oneself by requiring others to tiptoe with them. Long live the avatar and its virtual world!

It seems that, at least here on Earth, it is the human being, and the human being alone, that may deliver Spirit unto Spirit. The loss of our humanity will have its consequences.

Forget meditation apps. If today's smart-devices are to serve for anything spiritual these days, then they should serve as mirrors to reveal humanity's long-overdue date with evolution.

The claimed "spirituality" in the ingestion of hallucinogens is nothing more than a hack. Yes, one may break the habitual code temporarily, but that break does not exist off the platform upon which the code was running in the first place. Just like the code before it, the hack itself is a "doing something to" perception. Freedom from all programs can only arise in the non-doing.

Capitalism is an economic system that thrives on the free market. In order to maintain a free market, legislation must step in when market share becomes too centralized. Without this kind of intervention, prices risk becoming noncompetitive. It is for this reason that monopolies have no place in a capitalistic economy. Spotting companies bordering on monopolistic power is not rocket science; they stand out like sore thumbs in the marketplace. But what of the subtle monopoly taking place right under our noses? Not the monopoly on the outer, free economy, but the monopoly on our *inner*, Free economy. The issue here is not the *monopoly on production* but rather the *monopoly on perception*.

The transition from the Renaissance to the Age of Reason (aka, Age of Enlightenment) proved to be no more than the mere swapping of one God for another—from the god of Fantasy to the god of Evidence, of Fact, of Logic, of Witness. To be clear, this was a shift to the Age of Progress, not to the Age of Enlightenment, the *evidence* of which in your morning news feed. Where progress outpaces evolution, a do-it-for-me generation is bred. Welcome to the Age of Entitlement: "Enlighten me!" they demand. Alas, the industry of virtual freedom.

If one must think of Freewill as "freedom of choice,"
then it would reside in the ability to choose Freewill.
Freewill is a state of being, not an exercise of choice.
To argue its existence as freedom of choice will only
confirm its non-existence.

Childhood, as a phase of psychology, is independent of age, for as long as the human worships the "parent," or, better, fears self-responsibility, so too, will it worship authority over freedom. Give an infantile nation the freedom of democracy and they will inevitably implement a dictatorship.

There is a big difference between not wanting to be controlled and wanting freedom.

Choice and Freedom are conflated terms, the former merely an outer version—a cheap substitute—of the true inner. If one restaurant offers twenty types of soda, and another offers only Coca-Cola and orange juice, which restaurant has more choice? Clearly, a selection of twenty. But which offers a greater choice in quality? Twenty of the same is no match for two that are different. Unlike choice, Freedom is a matter of quality, not quantity. Be not deceived by the choices we are "given" in our free society, for there is an entire industry of politics and experience that is selling Freedom's substitute. Freedom lies not in the free marketplace of democratic consumption, but rather in the upgrade to what you already are.

Government runs the risk of being governed by
Big Tech. Same puppet, different puppeteer.

The lawlessness of today's tech-industry should come as no surprise, for the new American Frontier is the digital frontier, a wild west populated by silicon valley cowboys—bandits robbing the databanks—poised not for the Manifest Destiny of yesteryear, but for the double-dealing required in manifesting a new destiny.

To look both ways before crossing an intersection is an act of awareness within the physical realm. And what of the metaphysical realm? Make no mistake, your essence has already stepped into the intersection. Have you looked both ways?

Humanity has been worshipping artificial intelligence long before the invention of AI. The pious—searching for God—worships the scripture; the spiritual—seeking Spirit—worships the guru; the scientist—estranged from Nature—worships the abstraction. It is the data—not the Divine—that has been deemed divine. Beware of the new God in town.

If news is fake, is it news? If the digital cloud is underground, is it still a cloud? If augmented reality can only augment illusion, can it be augmented reality? If intelligence is rooted in compassion, can it ever be artificial? If Zoom is connection in isolation, then is it connection? Fake news, digital clouds, augmented reality, artificial intelligence, isolated connection: We are heading toward a future built not in the enlightened dissolution of duality but in the misleading blending of opposites.

There is a place where it is neither a glass half empty

nor a glass half full, but just full. But that place is only accessible having realized the fullness in emptiness.

In the dimension of depth, there is no distance—
union expands. In the dimension of distance, there is
no depth—separation layers. Flatness can only be
penetrated by lifting it.

Vulnerability houses an abyss of human depth. To remake oneself in a digital environment is to flatten the opportunity to know thyself. It is to "belong" to a flat world as a flat being, a "rebirth" into the avatar species.

Self-healing begins with the commitment to the
knowing that the pain is independent of the object
that triggers it.

Once the software knows you have taken sides—you "love this" or "hate that"—fuel will be added to your fire.

The question is, "Is there a positioning outside of this spectrum altogether?" This would be the only way to ensure that your fire is your own.

Honesty isn't always the truth. As one's reality is subjective, one need not truth to be honest.

In the phase of childhood, beliefs are installed. In the phase of adulthood, those same, held beliefs become "bought into," for is the transition from childhood to adulthood not that moment when, beyond innocence, wisdom rises as a potential? To miss this leap is to land on ignorance. "A programmed adult is its own programmer," says wisdom. What now of Mommy and Daddy?

Beliefs—the Christian in God, the Buddhist in Nirvana, the Nazi in the "Aryan," the citizenry in freedom, the follower in an ideal, the spiritual seeker in a path—are nothing more than a game of Pokémon GO: Projections of Pikachu, Charmander, Squirtle, Bulbasaur, and all the rest. History has revealed our murderous tendency to catch 'em all.

In this day and age, we must discern what is awe and
what is distraction. To brighten an artificial light is to
brighten artifice. Captivity is captivation's final stop.

The Soul seeker—as a seeker—is never home, for all seeking ends upon arrival. To confuse "seekers" as being "spiritual" is to label a lifestyle, an industry. It is to replace the forgotten-real by the consumed-fake.

122   If Knowledge is the answer, then there can be no question.

Presence knows no "means to an end," for, in presence, the mean itself is the end. All action is, in and of itself, complete in meaning. Put simply, there is no such thing as "running an errand," but only "running."

There is a fine line between the original and its versions. If novelty gets old, then it was never novel to begin with but rather a mind's substitute of the real thing. Real novelty is a flame without smoke, a gift that keeps opening. Its source of light is light itself.

In the inverse universe, deeper states of sleep are
perceived as awakenings.

The *natural* fall of man follows the *natural* curving of spacetime within us. Beware of those tampering with gravity, for they use this natural momentum to further bend spacetime into an artificial pull—a virtual gravity toward a virtual planet.

Soul Freedom is not only Freedom, but it is for free. That is how free it is. The moment we search for freedom or strive for freedom, freedom is no longer free but earned, and this cannot be true freedom as it was not for free. We grow up earning freedoms—freedoms granted by Mommy and Daddy, freedom to drive, to drink, to vote, to travel—but we confound this outer freedom for inner Freedom. We've eclipsed one over the other. The Spiritual marketplace thrives on the consumer's eclipse. Like a pickpocket selling your wallet back to you, it exploits the endless effort to earn what you already are.

Nothing that one knows exists outside of one's own memory. The known is stored, encapsulated, limited to the very dimension which it, itself, has created. On the contrary, that which lies outside this prison is the unknown, and it will remain unknown even once one comes to know it.

Progress is timeline-based: the update, the new program; another Tik, another Tok. Evolution runs perpendicular to time: the up-grade the off program; above the tick, above the tock.

The human is a powerful creature. Its habits create its habitat. Break a habit, change the world.

The brain, the doer. The Soul, repose. In doing, we sleep. In repose, awake.

The dream you will wake up to is beyond your wildest dreams.

About John Mack

Since the dawn of augmented reality (AR) gaming apps, addiction to social media and device use in general, thinker, writer and artist John Mack has been reflecting on the risks that the unmitigated use of smart devices pose to our humanity. Troubled by the innocent guise of intrinsically egregious software, Mack has deeply felt the urgency to alert and educate about the responsible use of such applications and the inevitable pitfalls for our future if we fail to rise to the occasion. In 2021 Mack founded the *Life Calling Initiative*, a not-for-profit organization aimed at preserving humanity's awe and connection to the natural world during an age of exponential digital distraction. Mack is a speaker at conferences and universities on the subjects of technology and consciousness and works to raise awareness through a variety of mediums.